Praise for
Your Ink on My Soul

"Christina Strigas writes with elegance but she sometimes injects such grittiness and truth into her lines about the melancholy of the past and of relationships. This is honest poetry. Her work is so honest and personal that you feel she's writing about you and your own experiences. She is a serious talent, a contemporary poetic voice that reminds me of the honest and sensual work of Ellen Bass."

—Nicholas Trandahl, author of *Pulling Words*

"I have never read a poet who speaks my thoughts right back to me the way Christina Strigas does. Whether she's writing about drinking shots of Metaxa and Greek coffee for six days straight or how his words were like scissors snipping the thread to let out her soul, I can feel every word."

—Chrissi Sepe, author of *Iggy Gorgess*

"*Your Ink on My Soul* reached in and tugged at emotions I had forgotten ever existed within me. And now, like any great poetry book, I find something new, something deeper, each time I read it and I want more."

—April Green, author of *Earthsong*

YOUR INK ON MY SOUL

Christina Strigas
YOUR INK ON MY SOUL

Written and Arranged
by
Christina Strigas

All right reserved under International Copyright Conventions for the Protectionof Literary and Artistic Works. No part of this publication may be reproduced, stored in a retrieval system, transmitted in any for or by any means, electronic, photocopying, printing, recording, online or otherwise without prior permission of the publisher, Christina Strigas.

For permission requests, email the author: christinastrigasauthor@gmail.com

Cover Art: Original painting by Christina Strigas, 2022
COPYRIGHT 2016 © CHRISTINA STRIGAS
ISBN 978-0-9951865-1-4
1st Editon, 451 Press 2016
2nd Edition, self-published 2016
3rd Edition, self-published, Copyright © 2022

Made With Love

Also by
Christina Strigas

In My Own Flood (2016) self-published poetry

Love & Vodka (2016) self-published poetry

A Book of Chrissyisms (2018) self-published poetry, quotes, inspiration

Love & Metaxa (2021) self-published poetry

for all the lonely hearts being pulled out of the ground (2022) Free Lines Press, poetry

The Wanting (2021) The Wild Rose Press, erotic romance novel

Crush (2021) The Wild Rose Press, paranormal romance novel

YOUR INK ON MY SOUL

CHRISTINA STRIGAS

A Chapbook

Contents

Introduction	/1
Misunderstand me	/2
Way Out	/3
Illusions of Handholding	/4
Crucify Ourselves	/6
1973	/8
Sixteen	/11
We are the same soul	/13
Breaking into a thousand pieces	/14
Yes	/15
Gird	/16
His book of poetry	/18
Elements	/20
Dimples	/22
One Thousand	/24
Waves	/25
What If?	/26
Frozen prose	/27
Captain	/28
Silence	/29
Contemporary Verse	/30
A beat in a drum	/31
So Feverishly	/32
One Thing	/34
Shades	/36
Times Square kiss	/37
On being Virginia Woolf	/38
Waiting	/39
Stay eternal with me	/40
A jail full of kisses	/41
The hues of light around the anger	/43
Writing is	/45
Mountain Daisy	/46
Last	/47

CHRISTINA STRIGAS

Introduction

This is my first chapbook published in 2016.
I had no intention of changing anything about this first chapbook, but everything in the universe happens for a reason.

It was time to freshen it up with new words,
light, and my art.

Art never gets old, it matures with time. It was time to revisit it, reread it, and add some new ones to the batch.

This chapbook is for all the readers out there who believe in the power of words and its healing nature.

Thank you for
reading my poems.

Misunderstand Me

Tears break the surface
You told me I was wrong
to all my rights
as I stared at tombstones
read ancient Greek adages
rolled in limousines
to graveyards and churches
but funerals are exactly like weddings
do not fool yourself
death and love
are interchangeable.
Wear black for white
white for black
only my mom is left now.
Coffin upon coffin of years
scan pictures to lost villages
escape time with movie star poses
kiss strangers into friends.
Drink shots of Metaxa and Greek
coffee for six days straight
and still the pain is not numb
it is all a farce this life.
Our bodies cold with painted
lips and pretty dresses or suits
to make a new home
stare at endings
make new beginnings.
late night philosophical quests
of broken dreams
unedited manuscripts.
Always doing what we could to
be understood
but all I want to do is be misunderstood.
Bury me with my books of poetry I joke
but I am dead serious.

Way Out

There's a way out
but no one wants
to take that door,
it remains open
for a while
you shut it with memories
reopen it after day drunk sex
afternoon delights came early that
year and same sex marriages finally
exist. There's a way out
but he wants to perform on stage
hold the microphone like it's me
sing to the women
about my heart
how it aches at worldly matters
that most girls barely glance at,
he whispered "there's the exit"
we took that door
it was raining hard on St. Paul street
he grabbed my arm
led me to this new club
we smoked everything back then
we kissed in dark shady corners
smelling like booze and smokes
red lipstick on his mouth duMaurier
packs in my bra
ripped stockings from his
fingers bathroom make up sex
we had rustic love
raw appeal.
There's a way out
of everything
you tell me,
and I feel like
you are as far as
the moon
and as close
as it feels
when I look upon it.

Illusions of Handholding

I get up
every mourning
to breaths of fresh air,
ran with my dog
in bottine avec talon
neighbours envious of
tight jeans and spunk
and no matter how many times
I leave, i always come back
to handwritten love notes.
Come back to his grip,
he knows how to woo me
how to kill me with words
when he holds me
I close my eyes
remember the first time
our eyes and souls met
our bodies never lying.
Yet he disappears
when my voice carries rain
he pretends i'm like the others
when my pain carries
splashes of colour
he never knew we could mix together.

he knows it all
thinks i'm easy
to manipulate into sewn fabric
but i rip too easily
shrink when touched
melt in your mouth
and i can't hold on
for much longer.
you're stronger
faster
wiser
and thus
i'm weaker
under the lies
i do not trust
the truth.
It shifts
into reality.

Crucify Ourselves

I don't know how some people meet once
and never again
they delete love like typos
it is a constant pain to love
the person who loves you back
who is somewhere in the sea.
i almost died and every time
i'm scared, i shatter inside.
certain songs make me cry
like a fucking baby, like the ones
you sent me. i never give up
but you
you never give up on me
i'm not 33, those years came and went
i have some numbness in my hand now
spent the day in the hospital
watching a loved one slowly die
and now going back for more
show the kids how death decides us
show my heart what love is inside of us.
you make it all better when they come
after me,
with lies and jealousies,
with hate and envy
you see me for more than a shade of plum
beauty that ultimately becomes ashes
and a thousand year old soul.

take me to that place
you begged me to go to even
if it does not exist.
somewhere in the photo
in the deep parts of my
ocean you float with me
and shut the door
to crucify me
against the wall
to kiss my tears
and bury your head
in the curve of my
collarbone.

YOUR INK ON MY SOUL

1973

I have authentic white tiny flowers in my hair
the way i was supposed to live
walking for my aunt, down the tiny cobblestone roads
in the middle of summer, following the gorgeous bride,
in the village my parents were born and fell in love,
singing Greek songs in the open air,
watching how the Mediterranean sun plays golden tricks
on my mother's short 70's crew cut.
It's 1979
on the plane with my dad
emergency landing to tend to the sick
his father is dying and everyone is talking about
olive trees. my hair is too short for Europe
my knees too knobby but everyone loves my accent
they say i'm beautiful
i sleep at the top of the hill with my cousin Mimika
and two other cousins have my name and moles.
I find it weird that we all look alike yet no one sees
the sun's brilliance like me
or notices how the moon shines at twelve years old.
they want all my clothes and look at the brand names
while i care more about the sky and my grandmother's sad eyes.
she likes to hug me like it's the last time she will
every hug feels like her last hug.
i felt death hug me when she squeezed and kissed me like that.
we sleep in the afternoon or climb out the window
to play with the hens.

It's 1991
everyone my father loved has died
I'm backpacking through Europe with my best
friend and we visit my childhood
but it's so long gone,
i slept all through Paros
Santorini saw all our dirty laundry
Pensioni Andre had no mirrors
so we hid well
under the sun's rays.
Every day lasted forever
every love a lifetime.
It's 1998
I'm three months pregnant in Agadir
and doing some kind of pregnancy test
it feels like this baby will live
and he does.
my life will never be the same again
i'm a mother
now.
It's 2001
the ultrasound indicates it's a girl
and i cry like a baby
praying she'll stay warm and safe
and never leave me stranded.
with blood and tears.
it's 2011
everyone sees Greece though the eyes of my
children and we love each other madly

YOUR INK ON MY SOUL

every year
every ocean
brings us closer
to death
and the cup we were meant to drink
together
and
finally alone
is full of memories
and our future is still
full of dreams.
he says no matter how old you are
you are always young to me
you never age.
i love you.
these are the years that grab me
make me cry to our song
and i sign death certificates.
i grab hold of my soul
and shake it a bit
then i silence it.
you thought you knew me
but truly it's 1973
and the sun is the brightest i've ever
witnessed and my mother's beauty haunts me.

Sixteen

There was a time in the 80's when I was sixteen
and Michael was my everything
while I was his nothing. And even years
later every time I'd see him he pretended
i was nothing. from nothing to something.
from something to nothing. i call him an asshole now.
even my daughter knows his name.
it's not a fucking secret how i loved him.
you probably never get over a love.
and when i left or you left or whatever
happened because it's all a blur,
for the second or third or fourth time
and i ran into you on the street
and you told me to stop my car.
you always wanted me back everytime
I ran you ran faster.
you married me we had kids
i had red roses and an Alfred Sung gown.
Once I met a man, it was brief,
maybe twenty minutes or so,
once he told me how my beauty
marked him. another time a man wrote
a book for me, he wanted my blood
as his pen sucked me dry out of my silence.
created some Greek fucking muse of abuse
and left me with ashes on my cheeks.
It's true that you never forget a love.
It's true that you love your wife.
It's morality to want it all and smoke in the hall.
i've lived it.
you have no idea how I live.

YOUR INK ON MY SOUL

I'm an artist and he supports my locked up
frustrations. my midnight madness
even if he isn't one, he loves my crazy.
But you, you get all of me
in a brown package
delivered straight to your heart and soul.
and you open me up gently.
just be sure
to not mix me up
with your other soul mates
and i will do the same.
my eyes and hair haven't changed much
everyone says i look the same.
and every love is you.

CHRISTINA STRIGAS

We Are The Same Soul

There are days when only your voice
can carry my troubles into safety.
I'm reminded of the eras we shared
it all comes back to me in flashes,
the waves we rode,
the courts we jested,
the letter we sent,
the cab rides we shared,
the way you told me
the only way to love is full of abandon recklessness,
don't you know silly girl that logic is useless
and reason is full of doubt
Then somehow my words get
trapped in your mind
and my soul is no longer mine
i shall search for my lost self
and find that little girl inside.
other times i marvel how you have taken
my wonder and transformed it
into poetic riptides.
The visuals of goddesses of
the past and present.

Breaking into A Thousand Pieces

It's not what you did it's that you did it at all
how you dissected me into beautiful fragments
of my soul.
no one else could do it like that
you took the best parts of me
and showed them to myself.
all my self-doubt drowned
at least for a bit until they resurface
when i'm naked in the bath.
you clutched all of me
with your tight grasp
and morning mantras.
how is it possible
to love like this?
to hate like this?
you will go one day
like everyone before you,
but for now
you can complete
the parts of me
that drowned.

CHRISTINA STRIGAS

The answer to your question
is yes.
It was on the tip of my dream
the way you weave yourself
into my unconscious
the words you use to endear me
sway me, bring me to your green side,
you know i'm there. all the other poems
mean nothing without you.
you told me this morning
how you love my beauty,
art and my heart
this is the message
the red trees whispered to me this morning
as I explained why the moon is still watching us.
you turn on my sirens to all my no's
and watch my lips say yes.
i'll be your little red corvette
been waiting decades to hop into your car.
stop raging against the words,
the world, can't stop humanity, can't stop gun control,
the Democrats, the Republicans, the Liberals...
the fight feels useless
leaves you powerless full of anger
that needs to be kissed.
Then i see it
the lion in the sun,
and it feels right
you know how fate needs some
kind of human intervention
for clearly
i would like to see your eyes again
perhaps live a lifetime
in a few hours
by the mountain
watch mother earth
perform miracles.
yes.

Gird

There was never a time for us
since you are the only
heartbreak I feel in every part
of my body. Dive into my words
let your soul swim
with mine. we will float
for centuries
but beware
of my love
it bites, and
self-heals
creates rivers
where forests end.
It can explode in
orgasmic verse
as sex and writing
combine
and I drink another shot
hollering at you
to write, motherfucker, write
and I scream at you
that no one can take my
freedom or my voice.
you say I'm glowing
and all you want to do
is touch my skin
in all the ways you've missed.

Come here and heal my scars
with your wounds.
Together in our silence
unite and untie these strings
this gird around my heart.
Come break me apart all over
again until my breath is yours
and my light
steals your voice.
This lil' heart is yours now
broke down all my walls
with how close
you came to my soul
just by uttering my words
for you
to me.
I told you, if writing hurts
you're doing it right.
and you realize this truth
so hold my hand
dive with me
into the depth
and mystery
of the ocean.
I know how much
you need me
to breathe underwater
with you.
I shall see thee there.

His Book of Poetry

There was a book of poetry
once written only for me
by my soul mate
and he said look into my soul
for ten minutes
absorb every word as a kiss
every sentence as a thrust.
my heart ached so much
i threw up,
my tears ate up my pain
and I thought he conjured
up Keats and the romantics
like he always does
and gave me their memory
as a gift,
circa 1890.
Chapters progressed like
Pablo and Mathilda
my love erupted
and soaked my soul
with bliss. Lost continents
were found
upon our love.
years meant nothing
i may have never seen him
(almost once)

fate denied it,
he didn't know about me
when he thought he did.
so i wrote a book
while he searched,
we missed each other by hours.
but his poetry
killed me
it struck my heart
and ripped it into
vines in a forest.
his love
and my name
on his lips
is tragic.
yet the most
beautiful world
we never discovered.

Elements

When you come back
you'll see how deadly
I bite.
I kept your secrets
as you kept mine,
it was an exchange
of the souls,
some that meet briefly,
others that depart hastily.
I may be an earth sign
but my heart is water
my soul is fire
my body is air
and your presence
is in my blood.
You should know nothing
is real in realms.
Every poem is a continuation
of the one only meant for you.
You love her so madly, It's lovely.
It's how a man loves
his dog and every woman swoons.
Still I read, you read,
it may be somewhat of a
variation thematic structures
unique to us,
but if I slip your mind
I promise to hang on
that steel step. Hope is
my downfall,
my rise.

CHRISTINA STRIGAS

I wait for you to slay
all your demons
come back from your hell.
This silence is madness.
In September I give most of what
I settle for away to strangers.
I'll cry if it's my birthday,
I'll shop at bookstores only.
I start to plant my new seeds
right about the 19th of September
as I lay naked,
in touch with my femininity
my masculinity,
swirling in hues of gold and
purples this aura conspiring with me,
as I take all my addictions
and drink them,
collect some poems
for my grave,
people like us, we're too sensitive
to the touch,
cry too easily.
Do you feel the words
on your lips, mouth, tongue?
Do you see how they hurt
when you swallow them?
This is why I must
regurgitate all of them
and place them
in my Virgo order.
My steel
becomes tragic
in it's element,
always because
of how I feel for you.

Dimples

It's a mad rush to the gift card
line no parking at carrefour
Laval
the kids want vanilla bean drinks
from Second Cup
and I want to avoid every single
person I know. This time death
dictates how sadness eliminates
joy to the world.
I walk into the lounge
and meet too many boys
asking me what I do.
I'm not easy to impress
with mediocrity,
I suppose ignorance is bliss
and the Greek philosophers
are so right,
but this whole scene
is oh so wrong.
It just appears to be fun
as my friends go for smokes
and I sit alone most
of the night
talking to myself
writing in my head
thinking of my comfortable bed.
Too pretty to be here

too old to care,
about what you do
or how you stare.
Purple lights and rain
ease the Cosmos and shots
numb all the fucking pain,
but you still slide into
my mind,
with your bad attitude and treasure finds.
You still reappear among the
vines in our make-believe forest.
You can come in and out of my life
like ink in my pen.
I don't want to hear
I'm beautiful
from strangers
I just want to
hear it
from you.
Yet I'm so drunk
I listen
and smile.
Cute dimples, he says.

One Thousand

In one thousand eyes
I could search for you
the purple sky
right at that time
when you can't
take your eyes off
the colors
even photos cannot
capture the life
of one thousand souls
to reach you
I could take the dark
keep it close
lose myself in its arms
but your thousand songs
comfort me more
I was born one thousand
times and all the while
it was you
I met again
to only meet again
under the thousand stars
that divide
us and connect us
bold or bittersweet
it has brightened
my universe
into one thousand poems
for you.

Waves

You have managed

    To open

        Up

            That part of my ocean

                That remained

                    Calm.

What if?

What if you meet me and you're not attracted to me at all?

What if I'm completely different from what you've imagined?

What if I'm everything, and more?

What if I'm a complete disappointment?

What if you're too good to be true?

What if your eyes are not as blue?

What if you're not who you say you are?

What if there's no magic?

What if there's too much of it?

What if I stop?

What if you don't continue?

What if it's over, before it began?

What if it began, when it was over?

Frozen prose

In my life, I want to walk toward you, as you watch me from afar, perhaps across a crowded street, or against a window, and when you see me approach, you think I look familiar, but you seem to be frozen on your seat, for you have seen so many women that have reminded you of me, but are you ever sure?

I walk without knowing you are even there, because I come to this city so often, it feels like it is just another street. At times, I think of you, of how we only spoke for a while, but never met.

It seemed there was always something stopping us from meeting; your lover, my lover, my distance, your home. When we spoke so friendly, so openly; questions led to more answers, until every word felt binding. A simple, yes, became sexual; it had so many implications. It took me a while to digest and give you an answer; at times, it was immediate. Urgent. Animalistic. Intense. Beautiful.

Suddenly, words turned into rhymes and you ripped apart all the seams along my heart. Your words were the scissors snipping the thread to let out my soul. I fought it. I ran. I left the country, and still you never forgot me. You spoke about magic, not as a song title, but as an ancient wisdom, an ethereal connection.

I moved to yet another country, with warmer climates and beach front homes. I remember how we analyzed the sky without ever looking into each other's eyes. We breathed and existed and shared our words on a daily basis like food.

Every day the same question…where are you now?

So I walk past you, and because I don't know you're there, I am oblivious that you are watching me. I haven't realized that the clothes I wore that morning, are the clothes you will remember me by. You know exactly who I am now, you knew from the first second. I never realized that what I so desperately wanted to happen, just did.

You have imagined this scenario in your head so many times, but something is holding you back. You cannot move, nor run, nor forget the hasty good-bye, the silence, this blocks your legs from moving as your soul cries out to you.

I walk past now and you see my back, the shape of my ass, my hair, as I fade away.
Years later, you will question if I even existed, if I even walked by that day.
I will keep you always as I had you, locked up in my heart.

YOUR INK ON MY SOUL

Captain

You dive right into me
as if I was the ocean
yet you have no fear
certain I will catch you
then you know
throughout
how I would take your hand
without a doubt
even if your words are quiet or loud
It is your voice I hear
even when my ocean is frozen
you find the passage to my soul
sail right into my very core
no other man has before
so I name you
the Captain of my soul
the sailor of my soul
the navigator of my body
the answer to my morning
afternoon
and night
questions.
You must know the lies the
made up truths merely
gaze into my eyes know
that I would travel water,
land or time
for you.

Silence

You shouldn't interpret my
silence the wrong way
I still want to teach you
everythingI know.

Still I see clearly
that in my soul
there lies a name
only I can read
and a face
I have never seen.

When I heard those songs
I thought how they were written for us
and crying and driving
instead of texting and
driving is safer.

All I need is a shot of whiskey
to burn my soul.

YOUR INK ON MY SOUL

Contemporary Verse

It was at the Baie de Pampelone
my heart was pulled out of my chest
and given to you in an antique cup
You said
I love your bob hairdo
I smiled at the word hair do
Do you drink cafe au lait?
Oui, I said.
I knew you had a gambit of tricks
you told me about a trapeze artist
who fell in love with a whore
your choice of topic
distracted me from my internal dialogue
about the specks in your eyes
I did rank them as the brightest
my eyes had ever seen.
I did not mind the neon lights
in the middle of the day
or the Rococo furniture we gazed upon
you spoke of Proust
as if you had seen him last week
Simone and Jean Paul were your ideal couple
the sententious attitude still did not dissuade me
I wished to relish in your fresh presence
record the hue of your eyes
as they rivaled the open sky
Would you like to take a promenade?
Mais, oui I said giggling at your
vocabulary as we walked through
a scrubby area aligned with pastel homes
and you simply took my hand
as if it was an extension of yours.

A beat in a dream

It is a rerun again
you woke me up
when I loved the way
you were smelling my neck
by the bathroom
like I was a flower
you wanted to cut and preserve
place me in a book
smelling the pages.
In that state you rarely speak
your eyes do
and they tell of your desire.
I giggled again
when you said I smelt like vanilla.
    Linken Park exploded
and your anger resurfaced
left me in a cold sweat
with eyes closed
I made my Nescafe coffee.
A man on the radio said he read books
when he goofed off at work
I knew it was not you
And still I wait for the signs
So I go back to sleep
And wait for your closeness.

YOUR INK ON MY SOUL

So Feverishly

You call my house and I run,
run to hear you say
anything, whatever comes to mind
I hear only you
and wish to talk to only your voice
miles away from mine.
You feel nothing for me
you will not pull my hair back
to kiss my perfumed neck
I have caught your
desire staring at me when you thought
I was not looking,
with your well performed role
of great friend
and of a lost, untouchable lover,
you cover it up well.
It must be easier this way
to have never wrapped my arms
around your back, never looked at your naked
torso never fought over
grocery lists and overdraft bank accounts,
all this turmoil
makes you act surprised to be near me.
I know the boiling kettle inside you
yearning to comprehend my limits,
my zones of pleasure.

Listen, I quietly whisper
you will never know
I am changing before you
to someone you never thought
you would crave
so feverishly.
You tell me to read between the invisible
lines alive in front of us
trying to trample on the lies
kept quiet
lying in the cupboard.
Would you like to bake that delicious cake
you liked so much?
Chocolate and pecans
with a hint of banana
you came over for coffee
we never brewed it
our clothes evaporated
at the entrance door
before we even said hello
I want you to know
I wore it for you.

YOUR INK ON MY SOUL

One thing

I am running out of lined paper
to express to you my visions
of an endless ocean between us
and a magical connection
illuminating the light which is so
distant unattainable
I see you standing next to the
post waiting for my car to approach
and my eyes to meet yours
I can just say one more thing:
I imagine us running so far and so alone
no one can stop this touch of our skin close,
electrifying and still.
Still as a curtain with no open window
to feel a breeze
still as a lamp on a table
only able to move by a human push or
touch come and see how still I am
and wake me up to a new morning
where I see your naked back
and rustled hair
where we drink out of the same coffee cup
and I will certainly walk toward you
and tell you about my day
and let us discuss Ulysses

and Javert and Heathcliff's
undying love for Catherine.
I know I said I would only tell you one thing
but it seems I cannot stop writing
and exploding with emotions,
stories and heartbreak.
I can talk to you like this forever
no response is necessary
just this paper and pen
my company and my witness
to the bridge connecting my words to yours.
Could it be I hear a voice so low,
so quiet reaching over to whisper something
but I hear the music is too loud
and I once again
imagine this sailboat ride over
the Aegean Sea
drowning me.

YOUR INK ON MY SOUL

Shades

When the shades are drawn
the quiet of the night befriends me
this is the part you enter
like a guest I have been cooking for
your image stays the same
body never changes
but you fall down from exhaustion
you are too heavy for my light arms
I cannot carry you
I speak to you instead
I tell you that you have the most
peculiar eyes I have ever seen
I am a mind reader suddenly
the dark is no longer flawed
it appears to be entangled in ashes
and upside down wine bottles.

I may not know your favorite color
but we are not eight.
Do I really care about those trivial things?
I should but the tombstone is behind me
now while you are up high in
your white chemise.
As soon as I see your laugh lines
I forget the tone of your voice
and your favorite expressions
so I accept my solitude
embrace the ashtray
and turn empty bottles right sight up.

CHRISTINA STRIGAS

Times Square Kiss

Kiss me in the middle
of Times Square.
among the rush hour.
the constant traffic that makes
this city ours.
let our picture be the
backdrop to some tourist's camera.
for we never existed.
just a part.
from different addresses,
cars,
bus stops,
train stations,
all these means of transportation
take us nowhere
near each other.
but the sky
is the same.

"Tell me the time you are going to look
at the sky today. I want to stare at
the same time."

"Let's do it at 6:30 p.m."

i want to meet
you right there
where altitude
meets latitude
meets souls.
the anticipation
of just a look was enough
to make it through
the day
until the time
i would
feel you closer.

YOUR INK ON MY SOUL

On being Virginia Wolf

once upon a time you talked back.
you held the door open,
then let it fall right on my toe.
just last year my green eyes held traces of the brown
you left behind. next year another
poetry book awaits on the coffee table.
a book about someone else that inhabits my body.
some stranger with distinct midnight
and three-forty a.m voices.
her whispers are so fine and low,
you'd think i would have noticed her beauty before.
it took some sea salt baths and warm
hellos to finally see her without my glasses.
i may wear barrettes like a ten year old,
but trust me, i have been a fool in bobby pins before.
i am pretty good at fooling people with a bag
of London tricks and lies.
late night eateries and cocktail parties are
the place you will see me and gasp
how every one eats out of my hand.
except you of course, your wife is calling,
she has your children as hostages.
your shirts at the dry-cleaners,
she keeps you warm and the butler shines
your shoes.
i am a distant abbreviation.
the one between the layered cake.
the delicious tart on your lips,
hiding in places you never found me.
you think i am a bore,
my hair outdated.
but my words well,
in that, i may be your one and only
goddess and for this reason alone,
i prefer the river to your love.

Waiting

I am waiting for everyone to read my eyes.
No one sees.
The day is halfway finished and you have entered
my thoughts like caffeine in my blood.
I see the sun and think about how it warms your face.
I feel you deep inside of me even when I don't want to.
Prose is like a techno beat non-stop in my mind,
to see past the notes, past the haunting memories,
past the car crash, the drowning, the renaissance.
I close my eyes and breathe
in your words to spurt forth my own.

Stay eternal with me

what else is there to do
but love you all over again?
from the beginning.
to the end.
i met you to meet myself.
as many brick walls as I hit,
yours is the toughest.
you make me feel that writing
is the ring on my finger.
you can inspire me
with a midnight caress.
to inspire the fucked up muse,
the storm persists,
and the words purge
you make me want to love myself.
give me strength to write
the next chapter
of an unfinished book.
it seems to continue
to immortalize our love
through stories and words
that flow like rivers with no dams.
the flood needs no protecting.
you saw my breakdown.
crying at every gossip girl episode.
what type of coral reef lies at
the bottom of my soul.
a place where we can rest in beauty.
loving each other in the dark till eternity.

A jail full of kisses

locked inside my head
as I envision your salty lips
barely on mine, behind bars.

You are a play on words
prying into my nights, neglecting my needs.

I want to think of all the ways
you'll never love me again

this new age could be breathless
but you choose to go back to your old ways

if cheerleaders are chanting laying their clothes
at the foot of your bed will you watch them?

I exaggerate all isn't that what writers do?

Isn't this how poets feel?
Way too much
way too soon

cut off from the real
dreaming of the people we will never meet
the unbearable defeat of oneself
even when I get what I want
most of the time
it is not enough

I can't tell you, I'll show you
I want more of what
you cannot give me

you will never want less of me
all this want and need

YOUR INK ON MY SOUL

to be alone in a jail cell
with no cell phone
no phone call
no computer
no book
no pen
no one to tell you how I feel
    only your lost voice
    in my imaginary ear
    thirsty for a tall glass of water
    a plate of food
    some sleep
    all this
    and your kisses

all along my neck.
    I always ask for way too much
    I know
    I see the future.
    It hurts.

The hues of light around the anger

Every day is a blur of the one before
and the one before that
and the one happening now.
I am changing the date on my journal
to keep track. For a while, there,
I stopped.
I felt darkness around the days
of the week, the mixed months
the abyss will never end
I don't know what will save me
from the drowning days.
Nothing really. My coffee is warm.
The longer I stare out my window
at my lilac tree, the colder it gets.
You wake up and want my attention
you make me coffee. You know how
I get weak when you speak
my language of love. It's still
a cloud in my heart. It could be
grey or crimson blue, or white
gently swaying and then you
crack the mirror.

YOUR INK ON MY SOUL

I'm out of my skin, I'm shedding
a new layer of your anger.
I must drag myself out of the earth
walk on planks
you want me to love you and I do
in the way I should not.
I know better by now
but the clouds
never leave
they hover
expect me to be my best self.
I'm writing in an out of control world
hurdling hatred.
You make me so tired
let's stay naked in bed
create our own clouds
dissipate the anger with our skin.
Even fantasy has holes
we refuse to mend.

Writing is

a rush of adrenaline
straight to the soul
whether you like to admit it
or not, drinking is the death
of reality
guilty of feeling
too much for you.
guilty of loving
too much of you
all that is apparently true
Is not.
i know what it means
to feel your sting of jealousy
when you intend to be sweet
and delicious like a pear.
you have it all wrong
when I promise nothing.
i can make you love on the rocks
balance on your bed with one foot
all the tricks you
asked me to do
i didn't even want them
all I want
is what you cannot give me.

Mountain Daisy

if you pluck my sentences
exhaust my vocabulary
release your blood hounds
you will bury journals
in open caskets
take a trip to my mountain
unleash daises
into my mouth.

Last

Narratives are the bed
I sleep and wake in
most days
zombie writing
mouth drying silences
to want to tell you so much
but words play the piano
they take a rainy minute
              bleed out the facts
all the love I missed out on
waiting to be embraced
yet all your eyes see
is my golden skin on lined paper
all your eyes read
are the punchy last lines of
my lamenting poems.

If you enjoyed this book please leave a review.

Let me know what you think.
Share your favourite poems on social media
or lend the book to friends.

Thank you for spending time
with my book.

I wish you all love and light.
May the Source be with you.

www.ingramcontent.com/pod-product-compliance
Lightning Source LLC
Chambersburg PA
CBHW050546300426
44113CB00012B/2288